P9-CDO-911

BOOKS IN THIS SERIES

DRAW 50 CARS, TRUCKS, AND MOTORCYCLES

DRAW 50 CARS, TRUCKS, AND MOTOR-CYCLES

Lee J. Ames

DOUBLEDAY

NEW YORK LONDON TORONTO SYDNEY AUCKLAND

A MAIN STREET BOOK
PUBLISHED BY DOUBLEDAY
a division of Bantam Doubleday Dell Publishing Group, Inc.
1540 Broadway, New York, New York 10036

MAIN STREET BOOKS, DOUBLEDAY, and the portrayal of a
building with a tree are trademarks of Doubleday, a
division of Bantam Doubleday Dell Publishing Group, Inc.

Library of Congress Cataloging-in-Publication Data:
Ames, Lee J.
    Draw 50 cars, trucks, and motorcycles.
    Summary: Provides step-by-step instructions on how to draw a variety of cars,
trucks, and motorcycles, including a Ford Thunderbird, cement trucks, and minibikes.
    1. Motor vehicles in art—Juvenile literature.   2. Drawing—Technique—Juvenile
literature.   [1. Motor vehicles in art.   2. Drawing—Technique]   I. Title.   II. Title:
Draw fifty cars.
NC825.M64A44   1986   743′.896292   85-13157
ISBN 0-385-19059-X
ISBN 0-385-19060-3(lib. bdg.)
ISBN 0-385-24639-0 (pbk.)

Text and illustrations copyright © 1986 by Lee J. Ames and Murray D. Zak

To Mark David and Hillary Leigh, my two grand kids!

. . . and thanks to Warren Budd for all his help.

TO THE READER

This book will show you a way to draw cars, trucks, bikes and motorcycles. You need not start with the first illustration. Choose whichever you wish. When you have decided, follow the step-by-step method shown. *Very lightly* and *carefully,* sketch out step number one. However, this step, which is the easiest, should be done *most carefully.* Step number two is added right to step number one, also lightly and also very carefully. Step number three is sketched right on top of numbers one and two. Continue this way to the last step.

It may seem strange to ask you to be extra careful when you are drawing what seem to be the easiest first steps, but this is most important because a careless mistake at the beginning may spoil the whole picture at the end. As you sketch out each step, watch the spaces between the lines, as well as the lines, and see that they are the same. After each step, you may want to lighten your work by pressing it with a kneaded eraser (available at art supply stores).

When you have finished, you may want to redo the final step in India ink with a fine brush or pen. When the ink is dry, use the kneaded eraser to clean off the pencil lines. The eraser will not affect the India ink.

Here are some suggestions: In the first few steps, even when all seems quite correct, you might do well to hold your work up to a mirror. Sometimes the mirror shows that you've twisted the drawing off to one side without being aware of it. At first you may find it difficult to draw the boxes, triangles, or circles, or just to make the pencil go where you wish. Don't be discouraged. The more you practice, the more control you will develop. Use a compass or a ruler if you wish; professional artists do! The only equipment you'll need will be a medium or soft pencil, paper, the kneaded eraser and, if you wish, a compass, ruler, pen, or brush.

The first steps in this book are shown darker than necessary so that they can be clearly seen. (Keep your own work very light.)

Remember, there are many other ways and methods to make drawings. This book shows just one method. Why don't you seek out other ways and methods to make drawings— from teachers, from libraries and, most importantly . . . from inside yourself?

LEE J. AMES

SPECIAL NOTES:

On drawing wheels:
Since many of the wheels in this book are angled and not perfect circles, I've used a "drawn from quartering" method to achieve the appropriate roundness.

"Faking":
When drawing complex motor or machinery detail, if you were to include every nut, bolt, spring, cylinder etc., it would take forever and distract you from being concerned with the whole picture. "Faking" is one solution. "Faking" is drawing in the general look of something as complex as an engine with strong strokes, dashes, dots, squiggles etc. that just suggest the subject. See below:

TO THE PARENT OR TEACHER

"Leslie can draw a Rolls-Royce better than anybody else!" Such peer acclaim and encouragement generate incentive. Contemporary methods of art instruction (freedom of expression, experimentation, self-evaluation of competence and growth) provide a vigorous, fresh-air approach for which we must all be grateful.

New ideas need not, however, totally exclude the old. One such is the "follow me, step-by-step" approach. In my young learning days this method was so common, and frequently so exclusive, that the student became nothing more than a pantographic extension of the teacher. In those days it was excessively overworked.

This does not mean that the young hand is never to be guided. Rather, specific guiding is fundamental. Step-by-step guiding that produces satisfactory results is valuable even when the means of accomplishment are not fully understood by the student.

The novice with a musical instrument is frequently taught to play simple melodies as quickly as possible, well before he learns the most elemental scratchings at the surface of music theory. The resultant self-satisfaction, pride in accomplishment, can be a significant means of providing motivation. And all from mimicking an instructor's "Do-as-I-do . . ."

Mimicry is prerequisite for developing creativity. We learn the use of our tools by mimicry. Then we can use those tools for creativity. To this end I would offer the budding artist the opportunity to memorize or mimic (rote-like, if you wish) the making of "pictures." "Pictures" he has been anxious to be able to draw.

The use of this book should be available to anyone who *wants* to try another way of flapping his wings. Perhaps he or she will then get off the ground when a friend says, "Leslie can draw a Rolls-Royce better than anybody else!"

LEE J. AMES

Formula 5000

Jaguar XK-E   2+2   4.2 litre

Gabelich's "Blue Flame"—1970

Ferrari 512S Racer

1975 Triumph TR-7

1977 Maserati Bora

Hot Rod

USAC Midget

Hot Rod—Gary Reymund's '23

1974 Volkswagen Beetle

1936 Cord Westchester

1936 Bugatti Surbaisse

1957 Ford Thunderbird

1912 Brewster Town Car

1937 Pontiac **Rumble-seat Coupé**

1974 Glassic Model A replica

1964 Ford Mustang

1964 Corvette XP819

1981 Cadillac Limousine

Modified 1951 Ford—low rider

Euclid Dump Truck

Refrigerator Trailer

Ford Bronco II

1974 Ford E-100 Custom Van

Nissan 4X4 Sport Truck

Mazda B2000 Sundowner

Micro Van—Subaru's Domingo

Tandem Bicycle

Road Racing Superbike

Motocross (Panasonic) with Piranha wheels

Panasonic 10-speed Bicycle

Suzuki ALT 125 3X6

Lambretta Scooter T-V175

Mini Chopper

BMW R 100RS

Francis-Barnett 249-c.c. Scrambler

Yamaha Virago

Harley-Davidson XLH 883 Sportster

Husqvarna 430 CR

B. F. Meyers Manx 2 Dune Buggy

Penny Farthing—1870

1898 Winton Buggy

Suzuki Quadrunner 125

LEE J. AMES has been earning his living as an artist for forty-five years. He began his career working on Walt Disney's *Fantasia* and *Pinocchio.* He has taught at the School of Visual Arts in Manhattan and, more recently, at Dowling College on Long Island. He was for a time director of his own advertising agency and illustrator for several magazines. Mr. Ames has illustrated over 150 books, from preschool picture books to postgraduate texts. When not working, he battles on the tennis court. A native New Yorker, Lee J. Ames lives in Dix Hills, Long Island, with his wife, Jocelyn, their two dogs, and a calico cat.

DRAW 50 FOR HOURS OF FUN!

*Using Lee J. Ames's proven, step-by-step method of drawing instruction you can easily
learn to draw animals, monsters, airplanes, cars, sharks, buildings, dinosaurs, famous cartoons, and so much
more! Millions of people have learned to draw by using the award-winning
"Draw 50" technique. Now you can too!*

COLLECT THE ENTIRE DRAW 50 SERIES!

*The Draw 50 Series books are available from your local bookstore.
You may also order direct (make a copy of this form to order).*

Titles are paperback, unless otherwise indicated.

ISBN	TITLE	PRICE	QTY		TOTAL
23629-8	Airplanes, Aircraft, and Spacecraft	$8.00/$10.00 Can	X ____	=	_____
19519-2	Animals	$8.00/$10.00 Can	X ____	=	_____
24638-2	Athletes	$8.00/$10.00 Can	X ____	=	_____
26767-3	Beasties and Yugglies and Turnover Uglies and Things That Go Bump in the Night	$8.00/$10.00 Can	X ____	=	_____
24625-0	Beasties and Yugglies and Turnover Uglies and ThingsThat Go Bump in the Night (hardcover)	$12.95/$15.95 Can	X ____	=	_____
23630-1	Boats, Ships, Trucks and Trains	$8.00/$10.00 Can	X ____	=	_____
41777-2	Buildings and Other Structures	$8.00/$10.00 Can	X ____	=	_____
24639-0	Cars, Trucks and Motorcycles	$8.00/$10.00 Can	X ____	=	_____
24640-4	Cats	$8.00/$10.00 Can	X ____	=	_____
42449-3	Creepy Crawlies	$8.00/$10.00 Can	X ____	=	_____
41189-8	Creepy Crawlies (hardcover)	$12.95/$16.95 Can	X ____	=	_____
19520-6	Dinosaurs and Other Prehistoric Animals	$8.00/$10.00 Can	X ____	=	_____
23431-7	Dogs	$8.00/$10.00 Can	X ____	=	_____
46985-3	Endangered Animals	$8.00/$10.00 Can	X ____	=	_____
24629-3	Famous Caricatures (hardcover)	$12.95/$15.95 Can	X ____	=	_____
19521-4	Famous Cartoons	$8.00/$10.00 Can	X ____	=	_____
23432-5	Famous Faces	$8.00/$10.00 Can	X ____	=	_____
26770-3	Holiday Decorations	$8.00/$10.00 Can	X ____	=	_____
17642-2	Horses	$8.00/$10.00 Can	X ____	=	_____
17639-2	Monsters	$8.00/$10.00 Can	X ____	=	_____
41194-4	People (available 9/94)	$8.00/$10.50 Can	X ____	=	_____
26768-1	Sharks, Whales and Other Sea Creatures	$8.00/$10.00 Can	X ____	=	_____
47150-5	Flowers, Trees and Other Plants	$8.00/$10.50 Can	X ____	=	_____
47004-5	Flowers, Trees and Other Plants (hardcover)	$13.00/$16.95 Can	X ____	=	_____
14154-8	Vehicles	$8.00/$10.00 Can	X ____	=	_____
	Shipping and handling	**(add $2.50 per order)**	X ____	=	_____
		TOTAL			_____

Please send me the title(s) I have indicated above. I am enclosing $_____.
Send check or money order in U.S. funds only (no C.O.D.s or cash, please). Make check payable to
Doubleday Consumer Services. Allow 4 - 6 weeks for delivery.
Prices and availability are subject to change without notice.

Name:_____

Address:_____ Apt. # _____

City:_____ State:_____ ZIP Code: _____

Send completed coupon and payment to:
Doubleday Consumer Services
Dept LA 16
2451 South Wolf Road
Des Plaines, IL 60018

LA 16– 3/95